The Other Side of the Mirror:

Excerpts and Additions to a Plantation Owner's Diary

by

Aileen Bassis

Unlikely Books
www.UnlikelyStories.org
New Orleans, Louisiana

The Other Side of the Mirror:
Excerpts and Additions to
a Plantation Owner's Diary

Ten Dollars US

ISBN: 978-1-959377-10-8

A previous edition of this book was published by Dark Onus Press, 2023, with an ISBN of 979-8-21-080128-9.

Unlikely Books
www.UnlikelyStories.org
New Orleans, Louisiana

The Other Side of the Mirror:

*Excerpts and Additions to
a Plantation Owner's Diary*

You have been having our rights so long, that you think, like a slave-holder, that you own us. I know that it is hard for one who has held the reins for so long to give up; it cuts like a knife. It will feel all the better when it closes up again.

—Sojourner Truth

Acknowledgements

"Possessions," *The Minetta Review*

"Mineral to Marrow," *Leveler Poetry*

"Questions for America," *Two Hawks Quarterly*

3 Diary Poems under one title, "Excerpts and Additions to a Plantation Owner's Diary," *JMWW*

"Portrait of The Enslaver's Wife," *Lunch Ticket*

"In Master's House," (re-titled, "Reading a Plantation Owner's Diary") *Poemeleon*

"In The Land of Second Chances," *Great Weather for Media Online*

"Breath," *Cease, Cows*

Contents

Diary quotes that are in italics are from
"The Secret Diary of William Byrd II"
(An 18th century enslaver, tobacco plantation owner and
the founder of the city of Richmond, Virginia.)

Foreword
by Chris Herlinger

Aileen Bassis showed me the first edition of *The Other Side of the Mirror* during a shared residency at an Arkansas writers' retreat in late 2023, far from our homes in New York City. I was terribly impressed and moved. I felt Aileen had captured something essential about the long shadow of history and the pernicious legacy of slavery on all Americans.

Re-reading a new edition of the chapbook you now hold in your hands, I am even more struck by the singular power of Aileen's vision – not to mention the haunted but restrained language she uses to construct her considerable and impressive poetic project.

Aileen has done this with admirable agility and fleetness: 17 poems in 21 pages, with not a word wasted anywhere. Each poem conveys the gravity, weight and damning power of historical significance and consequence. And each thrums with life and quiet, understated vitality.

First, about the poet's vision. Aileen's is history made manifest. Through the smart and careful use of citations from *"The Secret Diary of William Byrd II,"* the poet has opened up a whole world to contemporary readers.

This is the world of Black humans as chattel, their humanity denied and exploited by the likes of Byrd, an 18th century figure perhaps best known as the founder of Richmond, Virginia (later to become the capital of the Confederate States of America) and an enslaver and tobacco plantation owner.

It is Byrd's role as slave owner that grounds this impressive collection. From the very first poem, "Plantation in 1709," we sense the extremes of power imbalances. Byrd enjoys a life of ease and comfort – eating well (enjoying "battered eggs and pork,/ beef hash and buttered bread") and drinking well (imbibing French wine and apple cider).

His life is contrasted with the experiences of an unnamed Black slave woman. She "ran away three times" and when "night fell," was able to escape, having previously run away "with a metal bit / fixed between her lips" and punished by being confined in a shack, her hands and feet bound and tied.

The reader cheers the unnamed woman on. But there is also reason to pause, reflect, and maybe even shudder: did she make it to freedom in Canada? Or did she lose "her way / in the woods along the river?"

We don't know, as there is no telling "how the story ends."

Here we are struck by Aileen's use of silence – silence that the poet respects, never daring to speak for the victim, but that keenly affirms the slave woman's humanity and resilience. And yet it is also grim and damning: Master William, we are told, never even "wrote her name." This is not a quiescent silence but silence tinged with sorrow, grief and even horrors.

It is also a reminder of the double-edged nature of power as understood in the Enlightenment times of Master William Byrd – the nascent sense of democratic political power to persuade and influence, and the power a colonial (soon to be American) slave-holding class had to dominate, exploit and brutalize an entire race of humans.

I have spoken of Aileen's vision. Let me also praise her use of restrained but poignant language, with striking details that flesh out a narrative. These include "a rake lying in a field," the aforementioned "metal bit fixed between her lips" and, perhaps most memorably, mud becoming a shroud during the woman's escape, and the possibility that her ghost "wanders between cypress trees." This is haunting, disturbing and visceral language, but beautifully crafted.

If these poems take on the troubling dynamics of race, class and gender, they do so in ways that never skirt complexity. We are told in the poem "May 22, 1709" that Byrd's wife, Lucy, was responsible for the whipping of some of the slaves on her family's planation. The poet addresses Lucy in the next poem, a prose reflection ("Letter from the 21st Century") and acknowledges bafflement and anger. But she also expresses unsettling wisdom:

"I'm three hundred years away from you, and human cruelty continues," Aileen writes. "Genocides continue, refugees are herded into camps, groups of people are demonized, enslavement continues in different forms and Black and brown bodies are at risk for violence every day."

Not judging the past is impossible, the poet argues, but we are still left with "disillusion and perplexity" – the kind of ever-present realities that should give us all pause and make us look at the other side of the mirror in the present day, the present moment.

In a humane but pointed way, Aileen Bassis helps us confront the past and its continued contours and shadows over our lives as Americans in the still-unsettled 21st century – a moment in the history of a divided country when there is yet no telling "how the story ends."

Chris Herlinger is a journalist, author and poet who lives in New York City. He is international correspondent for Global Sisters Report, a project of *National Catholic Reporter.* He is the author of five books on humanitarian themes, most recently *Solidarity and Mercy: The Power of Christian Humanitarian Efforts in Ukraine.* (Morehouse) He holds three master's degrees, including one in creative writing from the University of Edinburgh. His poetry has appeared in *Newtown Literary; War, Literature & the Arts;* and *Bearings Online.*

Plantation in 1709

Master William ate
battered eggs and pork,
beef hash and buttered bread,

drank French wine and apple cider,
played cards and games with dice,
walked about his land

but he didn't give a name
to the enslaved woman
who ran away three times.

Once, she left a rake lying in a field.
Once, she ran with a metal bit
fixed between her lips.

He put her in a shack, tied her
hands and feet. When night fell
she ran again.

No telling how her story ends.
Some said she lived free up
north in Canada.

Others said she lost her way
in the woods along the river.
Mud became her shroud.

Some said her ghost wanders
between cypress trees. Master William
never wrote her name.

October 21, 1711

About 4 we dined and I ate some boiled beef.
My man's horse was lame.

A stop along a journey,
a traveler's inn,
a narrow room lit
by a tallow candle — fleshy scent.
       Footsteps above, below,
       a whinny from the stable
       — door creaks.

At night I asked a negro girl to kiss me.

Soft he calls — grabs her hand,
the grass-stuffed mattress rustles, ropes
sag. Her eyes flicker a yellowing light.
Down she bends to press plum lips
to bristles — tasting meat and wine.

A vein along her neck tightens
like a rein threaded through a ring
and she swallows as if her mouth
held a pebble digging down her throat.

Monstrous as a minotaur with a great
and nodding head, their shadow
rides across a wall patterned
with blind-eyed tiny flowers,
some blue, some red,
some pinker
than a tongue
that darts between his teeth.

Number Them Like Spoons and Forks

A man opens his eyes
to the sound of someone's hand
knocking on his door.
Hands shine the man's boots,
brush dust from the man's coat.
Hands pull out the man's chair,
carry biscuits to a table. Another hand
spoons plum jam from a silver bowl.
A woman waits for hands to pour
her cup of tea,

The man walks about his house and strikes a boy
for sleeping by the stairs. The woman slaps a girl
for burning a slice of pork. The man fondles
a girl in the hallway where it's dark.

The man tells a farmer that he can have
a body in payment for a debt.
Someone listening
in the doorway, covers her mouth
and moans.

3

Plantation Economy

Master
Wife
Son   Daughter
His Man Her Girl
House Slave House Slave
House Slave House Slave House Slave
Overseer   Overseer
Field Slave Field Slave Field Slave Field Slave
Field Slave Field Slave Field Slave Field Slave Field Slave
Field Slave Field Slave Field Slave Field Slave Field Slave Field Slave
Field Slave Field Slave Field Slave Field Slave Field Slave Field Slave
Field Slave Field Slave Field Slave Field Slave Field Slave Field Slave
Field Slave Field Slave Field Slave Field Slave Field Slave Field Slave
Field Slave Field Slave Field Slave Field Slave Field Slave Field Slave
Burn the Land
Hoe the Soil
Plant Tobacco Seedlings
Hill Soil around Each Plant
Weed
Prune
Top Plants
Harvest
Dry
Bale
Roll
Trade
Buy: English Porcelain, French Wine, Chinese Silk

4

Unrecorded

Names
of
Africans
Who
died
on slave ships or flung
themselves
into the watery ossuary
of the Middle Passage.
Who
will count Them?

Possessions

He wrote to me:

    Fidelia, possessor

        of the empire of my heart.

My dowry was my virtue,

    my father's promise of one thousand pounds,

        — my trunk of petticoats,

shifts, lace and linen,

        opalescent buttons

            on a milky shot-silk gown.

Tiny stitches pierce

        rows of ribbons

            on the hem of every skirt.

The tailor's girl

        pulled thread through sateen roses

        gasping open

and tulip petals folded tight

        and when a needle

        grazed my skin,

she whispered,

        Never mind. One drop

of blood won't show.

Dogs are barking in the alley.

       I know they sniff,

            they stray

and wine spills across

       a tablecloth

            like promises

that leave a stain.

Lucy Beats Her Girl

March 1712 I had a terrible quarrel with my wife
concerning Jenny...she was beating her with the tongs.

A name, worn
       like a cattle brand,
             (her Girl,
                   his Little Jenny).

You don't tell us if she cried or moaned,
       gasped or wailed curses —
             or was mute with every feeling

sanded flat or if her eyelids
       shuttered tears as she sprawled
             unbundled like tobacco leaves

drying until edges curled,
       crackled at a touch
             ready to be baled and sold —

July, that same year, you wrote:

Moll was strapped this morning and so was Jenny,
I ate neat's tongue for dinner.

Diary Counterpoint With Lyrics From "Ballads for America"

Song refrain: many thousand gone

no more, no more

In the afternoon we played at billiards no more auction block for me
and then cut some sage.
Then I set my closet in order. no more peck o'com for me

In the evening I took a walk
and met the new negroes no more driver's lash for me
which Mr. Bland had bought for me
26 for £23 apiece no more pint o'salt for me

no more hundred lash for me

many thousand gone, no more,

no more

May 22, 1712

My wife caused several of the people whipped for their laziness...I ate some boiled beef.

Displayed In the Richmond Historical Society

Cat-o-nine Tails:

Nine Knotted Leather Lashes

Oak Handle Oiled Smooth

Letter from the Twenty-First Century

Dear Lucy,

I read your husband's diary and drove to Richmond to see your portrait in the Virginia Historical Society. I don't know if it's the gulf of time between us or social class or different expectations, but I can't find a way past your painted visage into you, the woman.

I know you were young when you married. Only nineteen, your prospects were diminished by your father's infidelities and his bastard child. Your marriage didn't appear happy. You and William argued often. He was annoyed by your grief after your two young sons died and you were clearly frustrated, easily angered. You took it out on the enslaved people in your home. Had them whipped, burned one with a hot iron, hit others with whatever household item was handy.

I'm three hundred years away from you, and human cruelty continues. Genocides continue, refugees are herded into camps, groups of people are demonized, enslavement continues in different forms and Black and brown bodies are at risk for violence every day. I don't what I hope to discover by examining your life and William's — a way to understand people who stand by and watch horrors unfold? People who profit from others' suffering, people mimicking cruelty because it's easy and familiar?

I know your life will be short. You'll be dead of smallpox by 28 and two months later, William will look for another wife. He's good at moving on.

But there is some justice. He took on your sister's estate and debts after you married him, and those debts ultimately impoverished him in his old age. As the saying goes, what goes around, comes around or as my mom used to say, the good die young (I never quite figured that one out). Although I think twenty-eight is young to die, I can't really say you were good.

I know I'm being judgmental, and who knows what generations three hundred years from now will say about me and the choices I've made in my life but what's the use of hindsight if not to judge another's sins? Thinking about our world now makes my head pound. Your century might call that feeling heartache or even say their souls are suffering but I have no name for this feeling. No words to bear this weight.

Yours In Disillusion and Perplexity,

Aileen

In Master's House

Lye soap and sun can't
wash away one November morning
when a small brown boy,
a house slave wet the bed
and was beaten.

He wet the bed again in December.

How old was he?
Five or six?
His name was Eugene.
Master made Eugene drink
a pint of urine. Was it Master's
piss?

And did Eugene ever have another name?
Did his mother roll
vowels from West Africa,
call him her Amani
or blur and shape
the name Ndifi as her yellow-
white milk crusted in the corner
of his mouth?
Or was he taken away
so young that she never
called him anything
at all and the memory
of his warm weight
sat inside her and maybe
she thought of him
on cloudy days before the rain
when her knees and hips throbbed,

or maybe his only name was Eugene,
boy-child waking night
and morning in Master
William's house.

13

Portrait Of The Enslaver's Wife

Light folds around her   yellow-silk

          like a pillar-candle

Shadows round her cheek   curve

        between lips

   press below her nose

            On her left

     a thickened impasto

of fading paint

and varnish layers obscure shapes

and it's hard to see a dark boy

        in blue

        livery bending

brown skin   black hair without a stroke

     of light

to wash over him   so he remains

     vague as a   footnote

        in a language

that I barely know

Is he the enslaved-boy beaten

     by her husband?

Brutal is the imagination

        seeping through generations

like a sweep of paint   that could

      be   a smooth yellow

gown or a puddle

      of piss

        or yellow light

from torches waving   in the night

Plantation Daughters

Mollie calls   Agnes   Agnes
        hold your sister's hand
            bees are all around
English roses nodding in the heat
Agnes picked up a peach

           lying on the lawn
bit into its orange flesh and tasted
          rot dripping
      beneath its skin
she remembers another summer
          Mother's bare foot
almost-color skin   violet vein like a lazy
          thread of summer

once a mosquito bit Agnes behind her ear
          then bit Mother
Agnes wondered
      did my blood taste like Mother's
did milk I sucked from Mollie's brown breast

16

flavor me

      dark

as molasses from the islands?

Mineral to Marrow

Vitrine of muskets, pikes.
Six knives, a stained wool coat.
A confederate flag.

Portrait of the plantation owner
in blue satin — imperious crooked arm,
curled wig. Opaque gaze.

You can't read his expression
but move closer to find your reflection
makes you part of this puzzle.

Mineral to marrow, we're roped
together, beyond grace, in a knot
that cuts too harsh for metaphor.

How did it feel to own another?
The other day, a cop in Georgia
said, we only kill black people.

Breath

first is breath (remember a doctor
saying, "wait, don't push" and
you floundering on waves roiling
through your body, puffing in and
out until "now," and you push and
out slides a baby — purple tiny feet,
a grey-white cord that the doctor
moves from the baby's neck and
you hear a cry and know the baby
took a breath — life spread before
you like a maze of roads streaming
to a sea that is forever salt as the
waters that filled your womb) think
now of George's mother or Eric's
or all the other mothers that waited
for a child's breath until he's a
man and then his breath is lost and
you wonder how or what became
of those tiny milk-teeth, rolled
beneath a bed-frame, tossed upon
the floor.

Questions for America

is that you america
in a hallway
or hurrying down subway stairs
or ambling through the dollar store
credit card in hand?

are you standing at a bus stop
pulling up beside me at a stoplight
& driving off before the light
turns from red to green

& is this all yours america,
can you hold it in your hands ?
towers & strip-malls
shingles & vinyl siding & garbage mounds
black as crows pecking at the bags

— & how about the sky
america & rivers hemmed
with bridges and shores
split with train tracks
& I wonder how you're feeling
america— if your head hums
if your belly's empty
if you need a drink
a nibble
a man-sized meal

— taste me america
my salty sweat
my sweet perfume
my sticky crumbs

will you break me
with a snap like knuckles cracking
or whisper sleep tight & pull
the covers up? because I wonder
if you dream of me & maybe
you're wandering
in a tunnel cold as doubt's

fingers resting on your neck
& you can't see a beginning
or know which way to go

so tell me if you're still breathing
america
let me hold a mirror to your lips

In the Land of Second Chances

you always have an umbrella
and the ATM says your account
has lots of money, do you want
that cash in twenties or fifty
dollar bills? In the land
of second chances, black teens
stroll through a mall and stores
don't lock the doors and black
men lope through suburbs and no
one calls the cops and in the land
that isn't here and in a time
that isn't now, police don't
shove black bodies
to the ground and bones won't
break and blood won't stain sidewalks
but stay where it belongs, pumping
into each heart and arteries and veins.
In the land of second chances
air swoops into lungs
and out and in again
in a beat as constant as day
falling into night and morning
light strokes a hand across
each face and lips
move with words
that almost sound
like song.

When we look into a mirror we think the image that confronts us is accurate. But move a millimetre and the image changes. We are actually looking at a never-ending range of reflections. But sometimes a writer has to smash the mirror - for it is on the other side of that mirror that the truth stares at us.

—Harold Pinter

www.ingramcontent.com/pod-product-compliance
Lightning Source LLC
Chambersburg PA
CBHW070753050426
42449CB00010B/2455